A LITTLE

GERMAN

COOKBOOK

GERTRUD PHILIPINE MATTHES

Illustrated by RUTH BLEAKLEY-THIESSEN

CHRONICLE BOOKS

SAN FRANCISCO

First published in 1990 by
The Appletree Press Ltd, 19–21 Alfred Street,
Belfast BT2 8DL
Tel. +44 (0) 1232 243074
Fax +44 (0) 1232 246756

A Little German Cookbook

First published in the United States in 1990 by
Chronicle Books, 275 Fifth Street,
San Francisco, California 94103

ISBN 0-8118-1013-5

9 8 7 6 5 4 3 2 1

Introduction

Visitors to Germany leave with memories of hearty, delicious yet simple meals. Traditions and folklore and religious holidays are celebrated annually. On these occasions age-old recipes are still used. Restaurants and inns are proud of their specialties, which are reminiscent of the simple, home-cooked family meals once prepared by grandmother. The recipes in this book come from all parts of Germany – north, south, east, and west. Germans have hefty appetites for good food and this book contains a selection of popular recipes to tempt even the most diet-conscious, together with cakes and traditional Christmas fare. The dishes are easy to prepare, and are practical, economical, and good.

Enjoy yourself, and *Guten Appetit!*

A note on measurements

All recipes are for four persons unless otherwise stated. Spoon measurements are level except where otherwise indicated. Seasonings may of course be adjusted according to taste.

Frühstück

Breakfast

The basically simple German breakfast becomes special as you sit down to a mini-feast of steaming hot, aromatic coffee, accompanied by a variety of crisp rolls straight out of the oven.

There is always an early riser who is willing to collect these from the nearest bakery (there are over 200 different kinds of bread and a great many types of rolls to choose from). Creamy butter, home-made jam, and honey usually complete the menu, but in most hotels today breakfast includes a Wurst (cold meat) platter, boiled eggs, and even an assortment of cakes.

Of all the various ways of making good coffee I think the filter method is best. It is of course important that you buy freshly roasted beans. Choose your favorite blend and grind it down to a fine powder to ensure maximum flavor (allow 1 heaped teaspoon per cup). Filter it straight into your coffee-pot or use an electric coffee-maker. To really bring out the character of your selection add a pinch of salt to the finished brew. Serve it right away, black or with cream, and never reheat it.

Leberklößchensuppe

Liver Dumpling Soup

Soups have always been important in Germany. As they are usually filling and satisfying, they could easily be served on their own as a light lunch or supper. This is a favorite of my mother's. For the stock you could use bouillon cubes, but they are a poor substitute.

Stock

---

5 cups water
8 oz stewing meat, or either marrow bones or chicken bones
2 stalks celery, 2 leeks, 2 carrots, 1 onion, parsley sprigs
salt and pepper

Place meat or bones with the water into a pot, cover and boil for 1 hour. Chop the vegetables, add to liquid and boil for a further hour. Season and strain, keeping only the clear stock.

Dumplings

---

1 stale bread roll	*1 egg*
milk	*2 slices bacon*
4 oz goose liver (or any other)	*salt*
1 tbsp chopped onion	*marjoram*
1 tbsp parsley	*chives (for garnish)*

Soak the bread roll in milk and squeeze out, mince it and other ingredients together to make a paste. Form teaspoon-size ovals, and drop gently into boiling stock and simmer for 10 minutes. Serve hot, garnished with chopped chives.

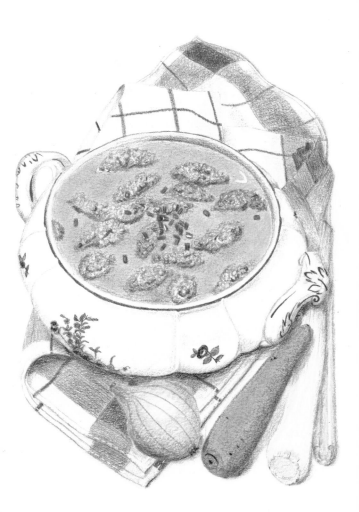

Flädchensuppe

Pancake Soup

This is another of my mother's favorite recipes for soup.

---

¹/₂ cup plain flour
1 egg
¹/₂ cup milk
¹/₂ tsp salt
lard for frying
4 cups stock (see p. 6)
chives (for garnish)

Whisk flour, egg, milk, and salt into a smooth batter. Heat a little lard in a frying pan, pour in some of the batter and fry on both sides until golden brown. Repeat until the batter is used up.

Cut pancakes into small strips and add to simmering stock. Remove from heat and let the soup stand for about 5 minutes. Garnish with chopped chives and serve hot.

Himmel und Erde

Heaven and Earth

This light and tasty meal from Westphalia takes its name from the
ingredients used – potatoes representing Earth and the fluffy layers
of apples Heaven.

3 lb potatoes	vinegar
2 lb apples	4 slices bacon
salt	1 onion (sliced into rings)
sugar	

Peel and dice potatoes and apples. Boil them separately in salted
water until tender. Drain and add a little salt, sugar, and vinegar to
taste. Put alternating layers of potatoes and apples into serving dish
and keep hot. Dice the bacon and fry with the onion rings until crisp,
and use as garnish.

Leipziger Allerlei

A Leipzig Medley

Originating in Saxony, this mixture of baby vegetables is an appe-
tizing accompaniment to lamb or veal, or it can make an attractive
lunch on its own. For best results use young, juicy vegetables.

8 oz each of: peas, small whole carrots, asparagus (cut into short pieces)	1/2 cup stock
	4 tbsp butter
	1 tsp cornstarch

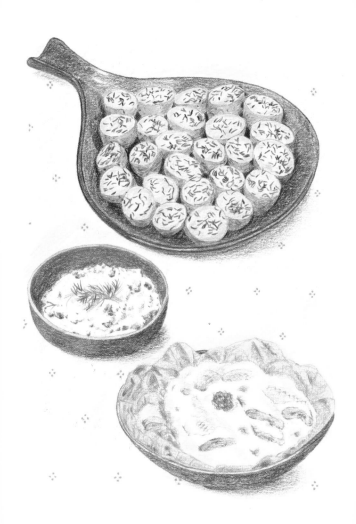

1 sliced kohlrabi	a little water
1 small cauliflower (separated	salt
into florets)	sugar

Fry lightly in butter, add the stock, cover the pot and simmer until tender (about 25 minutes). Mix cornstarch with enough water to make a paste and stir it into the vegetables. Simmer for another 5 minutes. Season to taste and serve.

Quark mit Kümmel and Pellkartoffeln

Cream Cheese with Caraway Seeds and Baked Potatoes

This is an easy "Friday night" meal when the week's work is done. It is economical and delicious too.

2 lb small potatoes	8 oz cream cheese
caraway seeds (to taste)	2–3 tbsp milk or cream
salt	chives, chopped
2 tbsp butter	

Wash potatoes but do not peel. Cut in half, dip the cut side into the caraway seeds and salt, place on a well-greased baking sheet with the seeded side up and cook in oven at 350°F until soft (about 30 minutes). Brush with melted butter. Mix the cheese with milk or cream. Add a pinch of salt and chopped chives. Serve with the potatoes in a separate dish.

Heringe in saurer Sahne

Herrings in Sour Cream

This recipe for the humble herring is simple delicious with rye bread or baked potatoes as a light meal, or, as an hors d'oeuvre, arranged on a bed of lettuce.

4 rollmop herrings	*1 small apple, diced*
1 cup sour cream	*2 tsp wine vinegar or lemon juice*
1 small onion, finely sliced	*salt and pepper*

Cut herrings into small strips. Mix together cream, onion, apple, and vinegar, and pour over herrings. Season to taste. Leave to stand for 3 hours before serving.

But remember, "Fish, like a guest, will stink after three days"!

Kabeljau mit Pilzen

Cod with Mushrooms

In Germany, fish is sometimes regarded as a distinctive meal to be served with elaborate sauces on special occasions. This recipe is simple yet has a certain piquancy.

2¹/₂ lb fresh cod	*1 parsnip*
juice of 1 lemon	*8 oz mushrooms*
peppercorns	*salt*
2 bay leaves	*¹/₂ cup white wine*

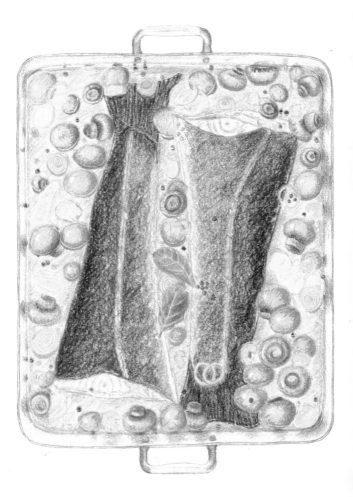

I stalk celery	*I tbsp butter*
I leek	

Clean the fish and rub in the lemon juice. Place in a casserole dish with the peppercorns and bay leaves, and let it stand for 30 minutes. Blanch the thinly sliced celery, leek, and parsnip and place with sliced mushrooms around the fish. Season and pour over the wine, dot with butter, cover with foil, and bake in oven for 50 minutes at 350°F.

Kartoffelpuffer mit Preiselbeeren

Potato Pancakes with Cranberries

This is a very old, traditional supper dish, loved by everyone I know. Serve these pancakes with stewed fruit or a green salad and eat them as soon as they come out of the pan. I like them best with stewed cranberries, but North Germans prefer them with sliced and cooked apples.

2¹/₂ lb raw potatoes
salt
I small onion, grated
2 eggs
2 tbsp flour or breadcrumbs
8 tbsp lard or oil

Peel the potatoes and grate finely. Mix salt, grated onion, eggs, and flour or breadcrumbs with the potatoes. Heat the fat in a frying pan, drop in the mixture in spoonfuls and flatten with a spatula. Fry on both sides until crisp and golden brown.

Sauerbraten

Beef in Marinade

This must be the most popular meat dish in Germany. Many's the time I've ordered Sauerbraten only to be told by the waiter, "We're" out of it"! The beef must be marinaded for three days in advance.

	2¹/₂ lb beef sirloin	
For the Marinade:		*For Braising:*
	1 onion	*5 tbsp fat*
4 peppercorns		*salt*
2 cloves		*1 crust rye bread*
1 bay leaf		*2 cups water*
1 cup wine vinegar		*2 tsp cornstarch*
1¹/₄ cups water		*1 tbsp cold water*

Place beef in an earthenware bowl with thinly sliced onion rings. Add spices, cover the whole with vinegar and water, and leave in a cool place for 3 days. Remove meat from the marinade and pat dry with paper towels. Heat fat in an ovenproof pot with a lid and brown meat quickly all over, then add salt and rye bread. Gradually stir in marinade. Cover pot and place in oven for 1¹/₂ hours at 400°F. Remove beef and thicken the juices with cornstarch blended with the water. Slice the meat and arrange on a platter. Serve the gravy separately.

Dumplings

Grüne Kartoffelklöße (Potato Dumplings)

3 lb potatoes	1 tsp salt
1 egg	croutons
1/2 cup flour	

Boil half the potatoes in their skins, peel while still hot and mash. Leave to cool, then push them through a sieve. Peel and grate the remainder of the raw potatoes, place the pulp in a dish towel and squeeze out excess liquid. Combine the mash with the raw, grated potatoes. Add egg, flour, and salt, and beat into a smooth paste. Form fist-sized dumplings. Press 4 or 5 croutons into the center of each. Drop into a large pan of boiling water and simmer for about 20 minutes.

Semmelklöße (Bread Dumplings)

This recipe is economical and easy to prepare and goes well with Sauerbraten. Dumplings are immensely popular in Germany, and usually accompany meat dishes. They may be boiled, poached, fried, or baked.

8 stale bread rolls	1 cup milk
1/2 onion, finely chopped	2 eggs
parsley, finely chopped	1/2 cup flour
salt	1 tsp baking powder
3 tbsp butter	

Quarter the bread rolls, and fry them with onion, parsley, and salt in butter until golden brown. Place in a mixing bowl, cover with boiling milk and let this soak in. Add eggs, flour, and baking powder, and work the whole into a soft dough. Shape fairly large dumplings and simmer them gently in salted water for 10 minutes.

Spätzle

Spätzle is an everyday pasta dish from Swabia, where it is eaten with almost any savory dish. These little noodles are considered to be genuine only if made by hand.

---

4 cups flour
3 eggs, beaten with salt
1/2 tsp salt and enough liquid (half water, half milk)
to form a very soft dough
1 tbsp butter for garnish

In a medium-sized bowl, sift flour, make a well and pour in eggs. Starting from the middle, mix eggs into flour, gradually adding liquid until you have a very soft dough. Beat and knead the dough until it forms blisters. Place it onto a chopping board and scrape thin strips of dough straight into boiling, salted water with the broad side of a knife. Let them swell up for 3 minutes, fish them out with a sieve, rinse in hot water and place them in a serving bowl. Repeat until all the dough has been used up. Before serving, toss the Spätzle in browned butter.

Schnitzel

Though usually associated with Vienna, Schnitzel has a permanent place on the German bill of fare. In Holstein it is served with fried egg as garnish, and in other parts of Germany cooks use mushrooms, sliced gherkins, or capers as garnish. I invite you to try one of many variations.

---

4 veal cutlets
1 egg, beaten
2 tbsp breadcrumbs
salt and pepper
4 tbsp fat or oil
½ cup stock
3 tbsp crème fraîche
slices of lemon

Remove bones and tenderize cutlets with a meat hammer (or ask your butcher to do this for you). Beat the egg and season. Coat cutlets in beaten egg and then in breadcrumbs, and fry for 8–10 minutes on each side in very hot fat. Remove from pan. Mix the stock with the crème fraîche and pour into the juices and boil for a couple of minutes. Pour this gravy over schnitzels, decorate with lemon slices and serve with a salad and steamed parsley potatoes.

Krautwickel

Cabbage Rolls

These are fun to make and very popular with the family. The common cabbage is indispensable in Germany and this recipe will enhance its reputation elsewhere.

---

1 medium cabbage
1 lb lean minced beef (or half beef, half pork or lamb)
1 medium onion, finely chopped
1 tbsp breadcrumbs
2 eggs
4 sprigs of parsley, chopped
salt and pepper
grated nutmeg
2 potatoes, boiled
4 slices bacon
1 tbsp oil
2 cups stock

Separate the leaves of the cabbage, remove the stalk, and wash leaves well. Blanch in boiling, salted water and allow to cool. Mix the minced meat with onion, breadcrumbs, eggs, parsley, and seasoning. Mash the boiled potatoes and add to the meat mixture. Place a large spoonful of the mixture in a cabbage leaf, make a parcel and secure with wooden toothpicks. Repeat until mixture is used up. Chop and fry the bacon in oil in a skillet. Remove, add to cabbage rolls and stock in a heatproof casserole dish. Cover dish and braise rolls in oven for about 1 hour at 350°F. Remove toothpicks and serve cabbage rolls hot with potatoes or noodles.

Schweinebraten

Roast Pork

After this Bavarian Sunday lunch an afternoon nap is recommended! Pork is by far the most popular meat in Germany. I can remember when our local farmers killed their pigs we were presented with a Schlachtschüssel (slaughter bowl) placed clandestinely on our doorstep. The pot contained a deliciously roasted piece of pork, several blood and liver-sausages, and Sauerkraut, the whole covered with thick gravy.

2½ lb pork loin	2 leeks
1 large onion	1 cup boiling water
2 sticks celery	

Seal meat by frying it on all sides in its own fat; then add diced onion, celery and leeks, and water. Cover pan and roast in oven for 2½ hours at 400°F. After 1 hour reduce the heat slightly and turn the meat to allow it to brown all over. When tender remove meat from the pan. Make a gravy by thickening the strained juices with cornstarch or gravy browner.

Sauerkraut

Sauerkraut is surely the best known of German vegetable dishes. It is usually eaten with pork, though it can accompany all types of poultry and game. It is generally most practical to buy it ready-made, as making it at home is a lengthy process. It is manufactured in large quantities and left to mature for several weeks in a wooden tub in order to achieve its unique flavor. Good Sauerkraut should always be very white and juicy. Of the many ways of cooking it, this is my favorite.

1 lb can or jar of uncooked Sauerkraut	1 small apple
1 small onion	1 carrot, grated
2 slices of bacon	1 potato, peeled, and grated
2 tbsp oil	salt and pepper
	water

Rinse uncooked sauerkraut thoroughly. Fry the diced onion and chopped bacon in 2 tbsp oil, add Sauerkraut, diced apple, grated carrot, and grated raw potato. Season. Cover completely with water and boil for 1 hour.

Kasseler Rippchen

Cured Smoked Pork Ribs

This is the traditional accompaniment for Sauerkraut. One might even dub it the national dish of Germany. (There is no need for salt or pepper.)

2 1/2 lb cured, smoked pork ribs (available at delicatessens)
1 large onion, sliced
2 tomatoes, peeled and chopped
1 large apple, peeled, cored and sliced
2 cups water
1 tbsp cornstarch
3/4 cup crème fraîche

Place meat in roasting dish, on a bed of onion, tomatoes and apple. Cover dish and bake in the oven for 30 minutes at 350°F. Uncover, add half the water and roast for a further 2 hours. Remove the meat and rub the residue through a sieve. Make a sauce by stirring the cornstarch, rest of water, and crème fraîche into the soft pulp and boil for about 2 minutes, then pour sauce over the ribs.

Salads

Kopfsalat mit Speck (Lettuce with Bacon)
Wash the lettuce and separate the leaves. Arrange in a salad bowl. Fry about 2 oz diced bacon in olive oil until it is crisp. Add a little brown sugar and enough vinegar to make a dressing. Pour the hot dressing over the lettuce and serve while the lettuce is still warm.

Fleischsalat (Meat Salad)
Sliced cooked potatoes, raw grated carrots, and chopped apples form the basis of this salad. Add chopped cold meat (Wurst), mix with mayonnaise, sliced gherkins, chopped chives, and tomatoes.

Gemüsesalat (Vegetable Salad)
Try this dressing, which is suitable for all vegetable salads.

---

3 tbsp salad oil
1–2 tbsp wine vinegar or lemon juice
pinch of salt
a little sugar
finely chopped herbs (chives, dill)
1 small onion, finely chopped
celery salt or pepper as desired

Mix all the ingredients together thoroughly. Try dressing with any of the following vegetables (use 1 lb quantities): carrots (cut into thin disks, boil until just tender, drain and cool), green beans (slice finely, boil until just tender, drain and cool), tomatoes (slice thinly), green or red peppers (core and slice thinly), cucumber (slice very thinly, omit onion from the dressing and replace with 2 tbsp or sour cream), beet (use boiled beet, sliced very thinly), celeriac (boil until tender and slice very thinly).

Kartoffelsalat (Potato Salad)

2½ lb potatoes	4 tbsp beef stock
1 onion, finely chopped	salt and pepper
2 sweet/sour gherkins, roughly chopped	capers or anchovies
4 slices bacon	2 boiled eggs
4 tbsp vinegar	watercress

Boil potatoes in their skins until tender. Peel and slice them while still hot. Add onion, gherkins, chopped and crisply fried bacon, vinegar, and beef stock. Season. Arrange in serving bowl and decorate with caper or anchovies, sliced boiled eggs and watercress. Allow to stand for a few hours.

Rotkohl (Red Cabbage)
Another salad which can be eaten hot or cold. It goes well with venison.

1 small onion	3 tbsp brown sugar
2 tbsp oil	4 tbsp wine vinegar
1 medium red cabbage	4 tbsp water
1 apple	salt and pepper
juice of ½ lemon	

Dice the onion and fry in the oil until crisp. Add the finely shredded cabbage, cored and diced apple, lemon juice, sugar, vinegar, water, and seasoning. Stir well and place in an ovenproof casserole dish. Cook in the oven at 325°F. for 3 hours. Serve hot with a main meat dish or cold with a selection of cold meats.

Labskaus

Savory Beef and Herrings with Potatoes and Eggs

This dish is local to Hamburg and Bremen. A traditional seafarer's meal, it is eaten at the launching of ships. Curiously, the name originates from the eighteenth century English expression "lob's course" meaning "fool's meat". It is, after all, a crazy combination of ingredients, but makes an exciting change from more conventional combinations. Matjesherring is available in delicatessens.

1 lb pickled pork (or cooked corned beef)	2 onions
2 Bismarck herrings	5 tbsp cooking fat
2 gherkins	4 eggs
2 pickled beets	1 Matjesherring
1 lb potatoes	salt
	pepper

Boil the meat for 1 hour in the minimum possible quantity of water, then cut it into small cubes (if you use corned beef, just cut this into small chunks). Cut up the herrings, gherkins, beets, and potatoes and fry the mixture in hot fat, add finely chopped onions, pour on the stock from the meat and steam for half an hour. Serve, arranged on lettuce leaves, topped with fried eggs and garnished with strips of Matjesherring.

Rehblatt

Roast Shoulder of Venison

Venison has always been popular in the densely forested areas of middle and southern Germany, but nowadays it is appreciated much more widely. Low in fats and rich in albumen, it is very tasty, though a little on the dry side. The meat should therefore be covered with slices of smoked bacon while cooking. A glass of brandy poured over the roast just before it goes into the oven enhances the flavor and creates a mouthwatering aroma. The venison must soak for three days in advance.

2¹/₂ lb venison (shoulder cut)
1 cup buttermilk
8 oz bacon
4 tbsp fat or oil
salt
1 small onion
1 cup water
1 glass brandy

Soak the meat in buttermilk for 3 days, then wrap it in bacon, place in the hot fat and seal on all sides. Sprinkle with a little salt. Slice onion and soften with the meat. Add water and brandy, cover pot and steam-roast in the oven at 350°F. for 2 hours. Serve with red cabbage and parsley potatoes.

Fastnachtsküchlein

Carnival Doughnuts

On the 11th day of the 11th month at 11:11 a.m. the Karneval starts in Cologne. It gradually spreads to the rest of the country, with each region organizing its own zany jollifications for this pre-Lenten festival. In southern Germany the Küchlein is the traditional Fasching, or Fastnacht, fare.

3 packages active dry yeast	1/4 cup sugar
1/2 cup warm milk	pinch of salt
41/2 cups flour	oil for deep frying
6 tbsp melted butter	superfine sugar
1 egg, beaten	

Dissolve the yeast in the milk in a large bowl, cover with 1 cup of the flour. Place in a warm place, and leave to rise for about 1/2 hour. Add the melted butter, beaten egg, sugar, salt, and the rest of the flour, and beat and knead to a soft, smooth dough. Leave again in a warm place to rise until double its size. Turn onto a floured board and roll out to a 1-inch thickness. Use a wine glass to cut out rounds, or use your pastry wheel and divide dough into 3-inch squares. Leave these once more to rise until the dough forms tiny blisters when poked with the handle of a wooden spoon. Lower the doughnuts into boiling oil for about 4 minutes on each side, or until golden brown all over, then remove them with a draining spoon. Place them on paper towels to drain off the surplus fat. Roll in superfine sugar and serve while still warm.

Heidelbeerkompott

Blueberry Dessert

Fruits from the forest are always a welcome change from the more exotic variety. My mother and I spent many happy hours in the tranquil pine forests of Franconia, picking wild blueberries, raspberries, and strawberries, and turning them into delicious desserts.

---

1 lb fresh blueberries   3 heaping tbsp sugar

Place the berries in a bowl, cover with sugar and leave until they have absorbed it. Cook very slowly over low heat until the fruit is soft. This method can be used for other types of soft fruit.

Apfelmus

Apple Purée

For this delicious dessert you can use windfalls. There is no need to peel them. Add cinnamon and cloves for a spicier version.

2½ lb apples   3 heaping tbsp sugar
½ cup water

Cut the apples into small wedges, add the water and simmer gently until the fruit is soft. Rub through a sieve and add sugar to taste. If you like, add a handful of seedless raisins and chopped almonds. Place the purée in a glass bowl and serve chilled with whipped cream, or as an accompaniment to potato cakes.

Frankfurter Kranz

Frankfurt Ring

For best results, spoil yourself and your guests and use butter in this recipe.

1 cup butter or margarine	5 tbsp cornstarch
³/₄ cup superfine sugar	2 tbsp baking powder
3 eggs	**Filling:**
4 drops lemon extract or	2 tbsp custard pudding mix
1 tbsp rum	1 cup milk
salt	1 cup butter
1¹/₂ cups flour	

Cream butter and sugar until light and fluffy and gradually stir in eggs, lemon extract or rum, and a pinch of salt. Sift together the flour, cornstarch, and baking powder and gradually add to the butter mixture. Spoon into a greased, ring-shaped mold (10-inch diameter) and bake at 350°F for 50 minutes.

For the filling, make a thick custard with the milk and let it cool. Cream the butter and mix it with the custard. To avoid curdling ensure that both custard and butter have the same temperature.

Prepare a crunchy coating by melting together ¹/₄ cup sugar and ¹/₂ tsp butter and stir until golden brown. Add 1 cup chopped almonds or hazelnuts and pour the whole on to wax paper. When cool, break into small pieces.

When the cake is cool enough cut through it twice, creating three layers, and spread filling on each layer (don't use it all!). Cover the cake with the rest of the buttercream and sprinkle the whole lavishly with the toffee mixture. This cake tastes best the next day.

Apfelkuchen mit Sahne

Applecake with Whipped Cream

This is a wonderful cake. It reigns supreme in Germany's coffee houses and is easily reproduced in your own kitchen.

³/₄ cup butter	**Topping:**
³/₄ cup superfine sugar	3 large apples
3 eggs	juice of ¹/₂ lemon
¹/₂ tsp lemon extract	sugar
salt	1 tsp unflavored gelatin
1¹/₂ cups flour	2 tbsp hot water
1 heaping tsp baking powder	2 tbsp apricot jam
1–3 tbsp milk	1 cup whipping cream

Cream the butter and sugar until light and fluffy. Add eggs one by one, lemon extract, and a pinch of salt. Sift the flour and baking powder together and stir into the mixture gradually, adding milk as necessary. When the dough drops heavily off the spoon, pour it into a well-greased springform pan (10-inch diameter with a detachable base). Peel and cut the apples into thin wedges, toss them in lemon juice and arrange them in a circular pattern on top of the cake. Sprinkle with sugar and bake for 45 minutes at 350°F. In the meantime, make an apricot glaze by dissolving the gelatin in the hot water and stirring in the apricot jam. Brush glaze over the baked cake while it is still hot. When cool serve with whipped cream.

Nürnberger Lebkuchen

Nürnberg Gingerbread

Nürnberg, noted for its heritage of art and architecture, is also famous for its Christmas market and gingerbread. This recipe from the Middle Ages received its name – Lebkuchen, or "cake of life" – from the natural ingredients and spices it uses, which were considered to possess life-sustaining and stimulating qualities. At Christmas, a gingerbread house is a firm favorite with young and old. The dough must be made two days in advance.

---

³/₄ lb honey	¹/₂ tsp ground cinnamon
³/₄ cup superfine sugar	¹/₂ tsp ground ginger
6¹/₂ cups flour, sifted	1 cup mixed candied citrus peel
1 tsp baking powder	**Glaze:**
pinch baking soda	2 tbsp confectioners' sugar
2 cups chopped almonds	and 1 tbsp water, mixed
¹/₂ tsp ground cloves	

Bring the honey, with half the sugar, to a boil and keep boiling until it drops in beads from the spoon. Leave to cool, then pour it over the sifted flour. Add the baking powder and baking soda. Knead to a smooth dough and leave for two days in a cool place. Boil the remaining sugar with a little water to a syrup. Quickly sauté the almonds in this. Blend the syrup and almonds into the dough as quickly as possible, adding the spices. Roll out the dough (about ¹/₂ inch thick) on a floured board. Cut into cookie-sized oblongs with a sharp knife, sprinkle with the chopped peel and leave in a warm place for a day. Finally bake in a hot oven, at 425°F, for 25 minutes. Remove from oven and while still warm brush with the sugar glaze.

Echter Dresdner Weihnachtsstollen

Dresden Christmas Loaf

Each region of Germany boasts its own distinctive recipe for the main Yuletide fare. This Christmas bread has been made in Saxony since the fifteenth century and is considered to be one of the most delicious.

½ cup (8 packages) active dry yeast	2 tbsp vanilla sugar
1 cup sugar	juice of ½ lemon
½ cup milk	1 small glass rum
8 cups self-rising flour	pinch of salt
2 cups melted butter	**Decoration:**
2 cups chopped almonds	2 tbsp butter
1½ cups mixed candied citrus peel	confectioners' sugar

Mix the yeast, a little of the sugar, and 5 tablespoons of the warm milk in a jug. Sift the flour into a bowl and make a well in the center. Pour in the yeast mixture and cover it with a thin layer of flour. Leave to stand for a few minutes; then add the other ingredients as well as the remainder of the milk, and knead into a smooth dough. Tear the dough apart and again knead it for a few minuted until air bubbles appear. When really soft and pliable let the dough stand for 2 hours in a warm place, covered with a dish towel. Halve the dough and roll out each piece into a 1½ inch thick oblong; fold the long side over once. Place both loaves on a greased baking tray and bake for 60 minutes in a medium oven (350°F). Remove from oven and while still warm brush with melted butter and dust with confectioners' sugar.

Christbaumgebäck

Christmas Tree Cookies

These make excellent decorations, especially when they have been decorated with different-colored icings. Choose Christmassy cookie cutters, shaped like stars, bells and angels. These cookies are really fun to make and the children can help with tying on the strings.

---

4 eggs
1 cup sugar
4 cups flour

Cream the eggs and sugar for 10–15 minutes. Add the flour. Roll out the dough on a floured board, and cut into shapes using pastry cutters (don't forget to make the small hole needed for the ties). Brush with beaten egg yolk and bake cookies in the oven at 425°F. for 10 minutes.

Blau Karpfen

Blue Carp

Carp is the traditional Christmas Eve dish, and is cooked "blue". The fish is not scaled, so that everyone can save one scale to bring them luck throughout the coming year. The fish's blue shimmer is a German specialty and is achieved by scalding the fish with boiling wine vinegar and leaving it to stand in a draft.

---

1 large carp
salt
2 cups wine vinegar
1 onion
a few peppercorns
1 tbsp dries herbs
2 oz butter
creamed horseradish

Place carp in a large pan, rub in some salt, and pour boiling wine vinegar over it. Leave in a draft for a few minutes. Bring to a boil in the same pan and add sliced onions, peppercorns, and herbs. Cover and place in oven at medium heat (350°F) for 30 minutes or until cooked. Rinse the fish quickly, first in hot water, then in cold. Return it to the stock for along enough to reheat. Place fish on hot platter, pour browned butter over it and serve with creamed horseradish.

Drinks

Man learns first how to drink. Later, he learns how to eat. He should therefore be thankful, and never forget how to drink.

In Germany wine is much appreciated, and so is beer, and indeed schnaps. Each has its place on the table and according to taste and convention is consumed regularly with enjoyment. There are many fine wines to choose from. Hock comes from the four main areas round the river Rhine: Koblenz-Rheingau, Rheinhessen, the Nahe and the Palatinate. Wines from these four areas have very different characters and flavors. Then there are the Moselle wines, made from grapes which grow on the hills alongside the rivers Moselle, Ruhr, and Saar. These wines should be drunk young and chilled. Franconian wines, from areas around Würzburg, are becoming more popular. Here are some of the most renowned German wines. Hock: Liebfraumilch, Rüdesheimer Rosengarten, Niersteiner Domthal. Moselle: Bernkasteler, Piesporter.

We mustn't forget the German Sekt or champagne – Cabinet Deinhard and Henkell, to name but two. They say that if you drink a small bottle of Sekt a day you will live to a ripe old age.

Like the wines, the many varieties of beers and lagers will help make your meal a complete success.

Schnaps, originally made by monks, who distilled it for medicinal purposes, has been produced for centuries. It is made from fruit, mainly cherries, plums or pears, and is still considered a remedy for biliousness.

Drinks

Neujahrspunsch *(New Year's Punch)*
In Germany New Year's Eve goes with a bang, literally. Every town and village organizes its own fireworks display which begins at the stroke of midnight and is accompanied by the glorious sound of church bells ringing in the New Year. Afterwards the revelers relax with this heart-warming drink.

---

¹/₂ cup water	peel of ¹/₂ lemon
1 cinnamon stick	¹/₅ full-bodied red wine
4 cloves	¹/₂ bottle rum
3 heaping tbsp sugar	lemon slices to garnish

Boil the water and simmer for 5 minutes with the spices, sugar, and lemon peel, add wine and rum and reheat to nearly boiling point. Remove spices and serve in warmed glasses.

Sektbowle *(Champagne Cup)*
This refreshing drink is ideal for a summer party on the lawn.

---

1 lb fresh fruit (strawberries, peaches, pineapple)
¹/₂ cup sugar
¹/₅ white wine
¹/₅ Sekt

Clean and slice the fruit, place it in a bowl and cover it with sugar and a glass of wine. Keep tightly covered for 2 hours in the refrigerator, then pour in the remainder of the wine and Sekt, both chilled. Prosit!

Index